What are....?

GLACIERS

Claire Llewellyn

Heinemann LIBRARY

For more information about Heinemann Library books, or to order, please telephone +44 (0)1865 888066, or send a fax to +44 (0)1865 314091. You can visit our web site at www.heinemann.co.uk

First published in Great Britain by Heinemann Library,
Halley Court, Jordan Hill, Oxford OX2 8EJ
a division of Reed Educational and Professional Publishing Ltd.
Heinemann is a registered trademark of Reed Educational & Professional Publishing Ltd.

OXFORD MELBOURNE AUCKLAND
JOHANNESBURG BLANTYRE GABORONE
IBADAN PORTSMOUTH (NH) USA CHICAGO

Designed by David Oakley
Illustrations by Hardlines and Jo Brooker.
Printed by South China Printing Co.(1988) Ltd, Hong Kong / China

04 03 02 01 00
10 9 8 7 6 5 4 3 2 1

ISBN 0 431 02378 6

British Library Cataloguing in Publication Data

Llewellyn, Claire
  What are glaciers?
  1. Glaciers – Juvenile literature
  I. Title II. Glaciers
  551.3'12

Acknowledgements
The Publishers would like to thank the following for permission to reproduce photographs:
Ecoscene: Graham Neden p.8, Andrew Brown p.10, Sally Morgan p.29; FLPA: Mark Newman p.6, p.18, W Wisniewski p.11, S McCutcheon p.17, Keith Rushforth p.19; NASA: Johnson Space Centre p.22, p.24, p.26; Oxford Scientific Films: Doug Allan p.9, p.13, Frances Furlong/Survival Anglia p.14, Kim Westerskov p.15, Godfrey Merlen p.16; Robert Harding Picture Library: Roy Rainford p.5, Kim Hart p.7; Science Photo Library: David Vaughan p.20, JG Paren p.21; Still Pictures: B&C Alexander p.4, Theresa de Salis p.12, Roland Seitre p.28.

Cover photograph reproduced with permission of Still Pictures.

Every effort has been made to contact copyright holders of any material reproduced in this book. Any omissions will be rectified in subsequent printings if notice is given to the Publisher.

Contents

Some words are shown in bold, **like this**.
You can find out what they mean by looking
in the Glossary.

What is a glacier?

A glacier is a river of ice that flows very slowly over the land. Glaciers are found in the coldest parts of the world.

This glacier is in Greenland.

This glacier is high up on Mont Blanc in France.

Glaciers are also found at the top of the world's highest mountains, where it is always very cold.

How are glaciers made?

Glaciers start in places where it often snows. The air is so cold that the snow does not melt. It piles higher and higher on the ground.

A lot of snow falls in the French Alps.

This glacier is moving down the mountain and into a lake.

At the bottom of the pile the snow is squeezed into ice. Over thousands of years, the ice becomes very thick and heavy. It slowly starts to move.

Sheets of ice

This **ice-sheet** is very thick. It is almost covering the mountains.

There are two kinds of glacier. Glaciers that cover the land in the coldest parts of the world are called ice-sheets.

An ice-sheet always flows towards the sea. Here, it breaks up into huge chunks of ice that crash into the water. They are called **icebergs**.

Icebergs take years to melt in the cold sea.

Valley glacier

The other kind of glacier is called a **valley glacier**. These start in small valleys in the mountains. They move slowly downhill.

A valley glacier starts high up in the mountains.

This stream is flowing from the tip of a glacier in Norway.

The end of a glacier is called the **snout**. The ice melts here and makes a cold mountain stream. Glacier water is always icy blue because it is so clean.

The surface of a glacier

The surface of a glacier is not smooth. There are many cracks called **crevasses** in the ice. The deep cracks show the clean, blue ice below.

The surface of a glacier can be dirty.

Rocks and rubble are carried along by the moving ice.

A glacier picks up rocks that lie in its path. The rocks move up to the surface as the glacier moves along. The glacier can move huge rocks a long way.

Changing the landscape

Long ago, the Earth was much colder, and glaciers covered more of the land. They scraped the land and changed its shape.

A glacier dug out this deep valley in New Zealand.

This **fjord** is in New Zealand. It was once a valley in the mountains.

The glaciers cut deep, wide valleys in the mountains. Some of these valleys have been flooded by the sea. They are called fjords.

Dropping the load

These huge rocks were dumped by a glacier.

Glaciers carry huge rocks as they move. When the ice melts, these rocks are dumped on the land. They may have come from a long way away.

Most of the rocks are dropped on flatter land. In some places, they have made high ridges and hills.

This small hill is in a valley in Alaska. It is a pile of rocks dropped by a glacier.

Fresh water

This river is pouring from a glacier. It makes a good home for many animals.

A lot of fresh water is frozen inside a glacier. When the ice melts, the water flows into lakes and streams. These are homes for animals and plants.

Mountain rivers are always full of water. We can use the **energy** of the flowing water to make **electricity**. Power stations like this one are built in the mountains.

The flowing water drives machines in the power station.

Studying glaciers

Scientists who study glaciers are called **glaciologists**. They measure how thick a glacier is, and how fast it is moving.

These scientists are camping on the glacier while they work there.

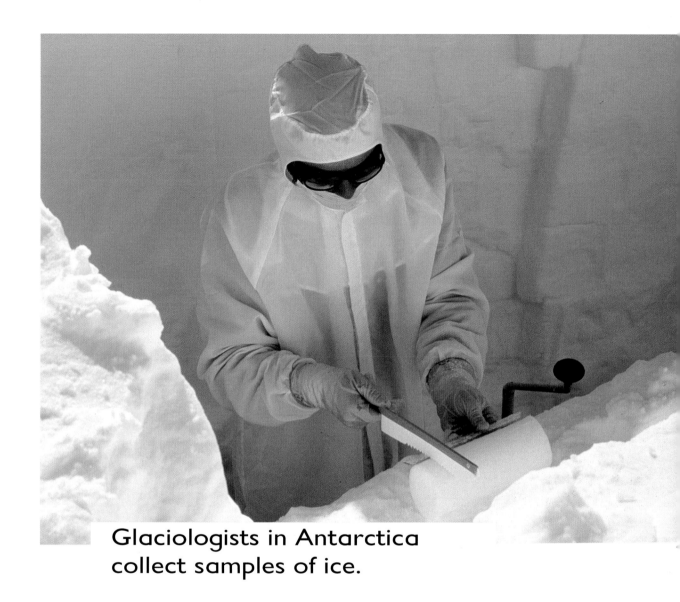

Glaciologists in Antarctica
collect samples of ice.

Studying glaciers is important. Glaciers
can tell us what the weather was like in
the past. They tell us more about the story
of the Earth.

Glacier map 1

This is a photo of mountains. It was taken from a **satellite**. There are **valley glaciers** in the mountains. The mountains lie near the coast.

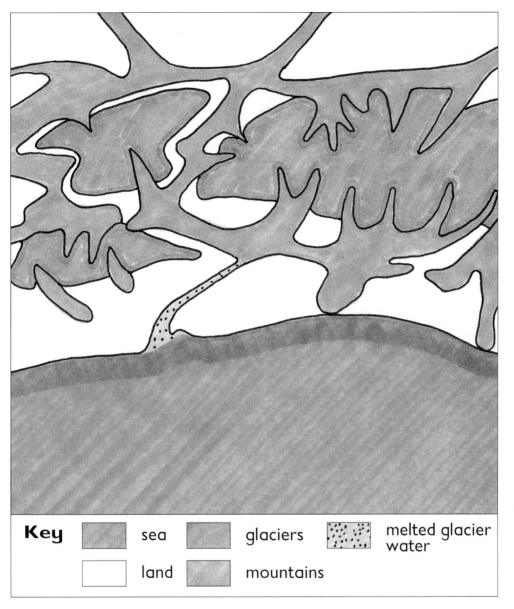

Key ▢ sea ▢ glaciers ░ melted glacier water

▢ land ▢ mountains

Maps are pictures of the land. This map shows us the same place as the photo. We can understand the map by using the key.

Glacier map 2

This photo shows the same place. It shows a smaller part of the land but you can see it more clearly. There are lakes on the flat land near the coast.

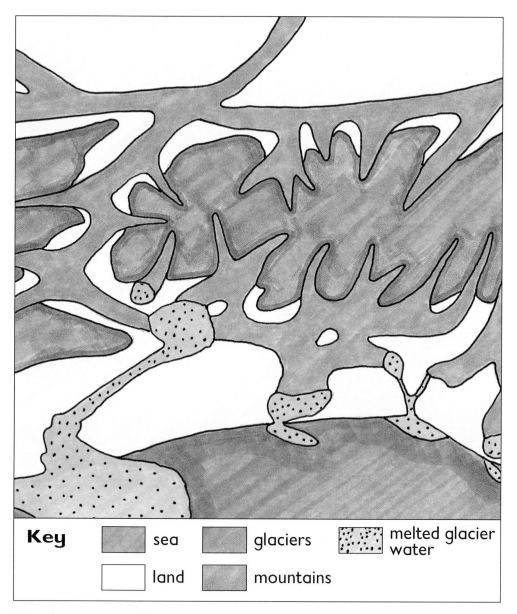

Key

▦ sea	▦ glaciers	⣿ melted glacier water
☐ land	▦ mountains	

Rivers are flowing into the sea. Some of the river water is icy blue. It makes light blue areas in the sea. This is water that has melted from glaciers in the mountains.

Glacier map 3

This photo only shows some of the mountains and lakes, but they look a lot bigger. You can see the glaciers more clearly. There is a lot of snow.

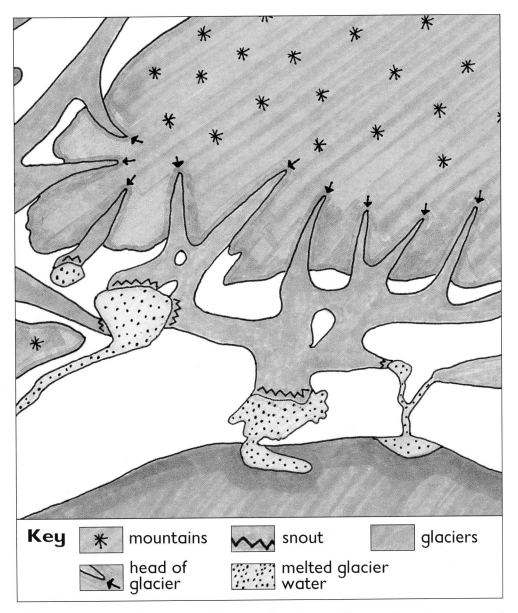

Key

✳	mountains
〰	snout
▨	glaciers
↙	head of glacier
⣿	melted glacier water

This map shows the whole of a glacier and points out different parts. The head of the glacier is marked with an arrow. The wriggly lines mark the **snout**.

Amazing glacier facts

The biggest **iceberg** ever seen measured
335 kilometres long by 100 kilometres wide —
that is bigger than the country of Belgium.

People can visit the Athabasca Glacier in Canada. They take a bus ride over the ice — on a part where there are no **crevasses**!

Glossary

crevasse   a deep crack in the ice

electricity   a useful sort of energy that can be used to make heat and light, and to power a motor

energy   the ability or power to do work

fjord   a mountain valley that was made by a glacier and has been flooded by the sea

glaciologist   a person who studies glaciers

iceberg   a large chunk of ice that has broken off a glacier and fallen into the sea

ice-sheet   a flat glacier that covers the land in the coldest parts of the world

satellite a special machine that goes round the Earth in space. It can take photographs of the Earth.

snout   the bottom end of a glacier

valley glacier   a steep glacier that starts in a valley high up in the mountains

More books to read

Andy Owen and Miranda Ashwell.
What Are...Mountains?
Heinemann, 1998

Miranda Ashwell and Andy Owen.
What is Weather? Snow.
Heinemann, 1999

Index